Victorious Couples

Melvin A. Jenkins, Ed.D.
Lael D. Jenkins, M.A.

Victorious Couples

Legal Disclaimer
This book is for informational purposes only. Neither the authors nor publisher make any claims or guarantees of outcomes or success. The content in this book should not be considered as counseling or other professional advice. Readers may implement the information included at their own discretion.

Editor/Project Manager: Spoonfed Motivation Publications
Cover Design: Daliborka Mijailović
Book Interior Design: Amit Dey

Victorious Couples

Testimonials

Victorious Couples has truly been impactful, inspiring and has encouraged us to be transparent. VC promotes the importance in spending quality time with your spouse.

Roger & Cheryl

The Victorious Couples group has given us a heightened awareness of the need for sacrificial love in our marriage. Our corporate prayer life has benefited as well.

Mark & Sharon

Victorious Couples has been a great learning tool to grow and fulfill God's purpose in our lives. This group has refreshed some areas in our marriage.

Matt & Quintina

Gary and I may have only attended our first Victorious Couples session but we have already grown from the experience and are looking forward to many more. It is a blessing to be surrounded by other couples where we can all learn from each other! God has given us all this amazing tool to increase goodness and love in our marriage!

Gary & Brenda

Along with the camaraderie we have built with the other Victorious couples, we have been able to reinforce the foundation of our marriage. When life happens, we can lose sight of our "Why". Through Victorious Couples, our dedication to unconditional love, selflessness and commitment to one another has been strengthened; it feels amazing!

Shon & Rita

Victorious Couples has enhanced our views on being committed to our marriage, serving one another in a godly manner and the importance of spending quality time together.

Roger & Marcia

Victorious Couples has been an important reminder that we are not in a silo. We've learned from others, both young and seasoned, and we've been open and honest, which has led to positive changes in our marriage!

Theo & Malaika

Table of Contents

Preface

Marriage is one of the most rewarding, albeit challenging, relationships between two people. Given the challenges associated with "two becoming one," it's no surprise that a wealth of books, workbooks, workshops, seminars, and counseling protocols have been developed to focus on marriage. In most cases, what has been developed attempts to address the difficulties that emerge after the ideals and attractions that drew you to your partner are a distant memory or forgotten. We take a different approach.

The Idea

As leaders of a ministry that has had a historically transient congregation, mostly made up of 18 to 21-year-old college students who after four to five years would graduate making room for those who will begin their college years, we noticed a shift in our membership base in 2018. Among the student population was a growing base of local residents who made this ministry their home. The summer months are a more relaxed time in the church and there are far fewer students around. While considering fellowship opportunities for the summer, an idea dropped into the heart of the Pastor.

The marriages among our local resident members range from less than a year to over 40 years and we had not really done anything focused on our married couples over an extended period. The summer seemed like the ideal time to bring them together to discuss various issues that arise in a marriage. There was some concern about the varying stages and years of marriages among the group. Rather than allow this to be a hindrance, we decided to apply biblical principles to support those differences and "level the playing field".

The Implementation

The first meeting was successful. Lesson one generated an energetic discussion. It inspired participants and they verbalized ways to adjust their perspectives around marriage. The word spread, interest increased, and the group began to grow, as did the vision.

By the second meeting, "Victorious Couples" was born. The original concern surrounding the various lengths of marriage dissipated. The lessons are appropriate and applicable to all stages and years in a marriage.

While uncomplicated, the lessons are thought-provoking and they minimize lecturing. Action and accountability are emphasized (James 1:22, 2:17). A by-product of this group is that it builds community and friendships. Incorporating technology into this process adds an element of accountability, comradery, and fun.

The Intent

This workbook is a tangible demonstration of the process we took our married couples through resulting in greater levels of intimacy, transparency, commitment, and peace. It is **not** meant for couples in crisis and/ or contemplating divorce. If that is your situation, we recommend you seek professional help from a licensed marriage and family therapist. It is, however, designed for those wanting to maintain, enhance or improve their covenant relationship... those who desire VICTORY!

Introduction

Congratulations! You are about to undertake a marriage experience unique in its simplicity, yet very effective in bringing couples together for the purpose of improving and maintaining their marriages. You will be challenged, encouraged, and pressed into making your marriage a priority, thereby fulfilling God's mandate that the "two shall become one" (Matthew 19:5).

When I first introduced the concept of Victorious Couples, a woman asked me to clarify whether the title had a double meaning. As I sought to understand her question, we discovered that she thought I was saying "Victoria's Couples," borrowing from a rather famous women's lingerie company. We both laughed as I quickly replied, "That could be an outcome if you and your husband follow the guidelines of the program."

So, what is Victorious Couples? It is a small group of dedicated married couples united by a bond of commitment to improve their marriages. The group can number anywhere from three to ten couples, and from newly married to more seasoned couples. (If you are newly married and don't feel you need this group, just sit back and absorb the rich information that you'll likely find useful in the future. Remember, a wise person prepares for the storm before it comes.)

Once you form your group and agree to meet for the first time, the following expectations are presented:

1. **All participating couples agree to meet/fellowship together monthly as a group**, usually over a meal. Attendance is limited to leaders and participants in your Victorious Couples group only—no children or visitors.

2. **Each couple agrees to engage in a weekly dating experience**. The weekly date does not have to have any expense associated with it (e.g., taking a morning or evening stroll around the neighborhood, window shopping on a main street, a picnic lunch at the beach/park, etc.). The date must be outside your place of residence and is limited to just the two of you. Couples are asked to be accountable by documenting (take a selfie!) their weekly dates according to #3 below.

3. To ensure accountability, **we ask all couples taking part to join a group sharing platform**, such as GroupMe or Messenger. On the platform, we share pictures of our weekly dates, exchange ideas, and plan future events. We like to use an app called "GroupMe" which enables couples to chat and post pictures of their events/activities. This is a great way to remain accountable in the digital age! Again, your group will contain only those couples with whom you fellowship monthly.

During the first meeting, the ground rules described above are agreed to. It is understood that everyone is busy with work, church, family and other obligations. These obligations can take a toll on a marriage or even contribute to its neglect. Since it is so easy to lose momentum, a commitment to meeting regularly is a must. One time per month is not too invasive and can keep the group alive. The best day of the week can vary depending on everyone's schedules. We have found that

Sundays after church work well for our group in Pennsylvania: we're already committed to attend church together from 11:00 am to 1:00 pm, and it's a good day for self-reflection and feeding our spirits to prepare for the week ahead. With this in mind, we decided that Sunday was a good day to also invest in our marriages.

During your meetings, it's important that the atmosphere be comfortable, safe, relaxed and free from distractions. There is no better way to create this environment than to combine healthy fellowship with a good meal. In the 1980s, churches frequently held potluck dinners. The thought of these types of dinners may bring back many memories. Borrowing from this throwback concept, we recommend you establish a "controlled" potluck dinner. A controlled potluck has a pre-developed menu and each couple contributes an item from that menu. That way you can avoid eating manicotti with potato salad (smile). Some groups prefer to have a catered meal; others meet at restaurants. Regardless of the group's preference, enjoying a meal together is a great way to begin each meeting.

Victorious Couples meetings are appropriate for adults only. We highly recommend that parents find childcare arrangements. To establish a sense of security, we modify a familiar advertising quote, "What happens in Victorious Couples, stays in Victorious Couples." To be effective, we must be open and honest with one another in our meetings. The concern that our "business" could be made public will place a chilling effect on our willingness to participate. Therefore, confidentiality is required and there must be a verbal agreement to adhere to this policy among all members.

One of the purposes of Victorious Couples is to show that there are more similarities between us than differences. We strive to become a marriage community that conveys the spirit of the roller coaster ride:

We are all on this roller coaster ride of matrimony together–holding hands as we push up the inclines, experiencing the fear of being too high, sometimes regretting that we got on the ride, and then releasing all our emotions as we scream together on the way down. In the end, however, we breathe a sigh of relief and realize that we made it through a very tough experience, ready to take on another ride. For most people experiencing this ride may be challenging, but well worth the price of admission!

Victorious Couples operates with one lead couple who act as facilitators to (1) guide participants through this workbook, (2) present scriptures related to the various topics, (3) encourage and direct discussions, and (4) share the assignments. Facilitators must also make sure members follow the group rules and maintain an atmosphere where all are comfortable to share.

Another important component of Victorious Couples is action. The lessons taught must be implemented. The assignments, while simple and achievable, will have tremendous long-term benefits if taken prayerfully and seriously. Relationship strife, jobs, children and life can interfere with completing monthly assignments. During the meetings, each couple should be prepared to take a turn reporting successes or failures since the previous meeting. This process helps the group develop a level of accountability. That said, the group facilitators must ensure there is an atmosphere devoid of judgment. Having an atmosphere free of judgment will help promote open dialogue and spread the love of God.

Victorious Couples is based on what God says about marriage. We believe that marriage is an example of Christ's relationship with the Church, according to Ephesians 5:31-32. We believe that a man who finds a wife finds a good thing, and obtains God's favor, according to Proverbs 18:22. The list could go on and on, but the idea is clear.

Accountability

A lthough we are all ultimately accountable to God, it is important to know that He gave us one another to help facilitate the process. In fact, we are all accountability partners on earth as God's ambassadors for one another. In many ways, our accountability to God is measured by our accountability to each other. A good scriptural example can be found in the book of James. We all know that God is the one who forgives and heals, yet He tells us to "confess our trespasses to one another, and pray for one another" for healing (James 5:16a). This is accountability in action.

Within the institution of marriage, accountability works in two ways. First, there is what I like to call *intra-relational accountability*, where spouses are accountable to each other. An example of this would be the husband making sure to let his wife know that he would be late coming home and why. Or, a wife telling her husband right away that she inadvertently overspent on the credit card. Intra-relational accountability can and likely does happen regularly and is a necessary part of the marriage experience. Failure to maintain it can lead to significant problems over time. In other words, there is nothing wrong with practicing the 4 W's without being asked, "Who, What, When, Where". Who are you with? What are you doing? When will you be home? Where are you?

The second type of accountability to consider is known as *inter-relational accountability*. This is when married couple A and married couple B voluntarily agree to hold each other accountable *as couples*. This is far more complex and requires that all parties willingly and intentionally agree to participate. I can almost hear some reader asking, "Is this principle of inter-relational accountability scripturally-based?" Of course, it is!

To understand the scriptural underpinnings of inter-relational account-ability, one must first consider the following three scriptures:

1. Two *are* better than one, because they have a good reward for their labor. For if they fall, one will lift up his companion. But woe to him *who is* alone when he falls, For *he has* no one to help him up. (Ecclesiastes 4:9-10)

2. As iron sharpens iron, so a man sharpens the countenance of his friend. (Proverbs 27:17)

3. Again I say to you that if two of you agree on earth concerning anything that they ask, it will be done for them by My Father in heaven. For where two or three are gathered together in My name, I am there in the midst of them. (Matthew 18:19-20)

As we look at these passages from a traditional perspective, we usually envision our Lord speaking to or about individuals (i.e., one individual person) in every case. While this is true, there is another perspective to consider concerning marriage. Let's consider how God views marriage:

> [4]And He answered and said to them, "Have you not read that He who made *them* at the beginning 'made them male and female,' [5]and said, 'For this reason a man shall leave his father and mother and be joined to his wife, and the two shall become one flesh'? [6]So then, they are no longer two but one flesh. Therefore what God has joined together, let not man separate." (Matthew 19:4-6)

In the eyes of the Lord, every married couple is *one entity*. When God joins a woman and a man in marriage, He sees *two* becoming *one*. He no longer sees the married couple as individuals, rather, He looks upon them as one unit. It's a little challenging for our finite minds to grasp, but it's the way God set up the mystery of marriage. Take a moment to go back and read the three scriptures above, but this time insert the words "marriage" and "marriages" after the words "one" and "two". As you do so, you will begin to understand the concept of inter-relational accountability. Can you now see how God has set us up for success, provided we are open and honest and accountable to other Godly married couples?

Perhaps you are wondering how this can be done given our busy lives and multiple responsibilities. Let me tell you how we're trying to facilitate inter-relational accountability in this fast-paced, digital society. In addition to regular in-person meetings as married couples, we are now using social media to supplement our practice of being accountable to one another. I believe that the use of social media is a good way for people to stay in touch, particularly over moderate to long distances, and while it has its negative aspects, social media can be used for positive purposes and is available for free to us all.

One example of how we use social media is through group chats, where we share triumphs and challenges. And, to make sure we keep our promises to go on dates weekly, we share selfies of our outings with other couples in the group. These digital images hold us accountable and enable us to receive feedback in real-time.

Before proceeding, be sure that everyone is up-to-date with their group sharing apps and digital devices. Be creative and enjoy sharing your experiences with your fellow couples.

Discussion

Group:

1. Discuss the concept and importance of being accountable in your marriage.

Couple:

1. On a scale of 1 through 5, 5 being very accountable and 1 not at all accountable, rate the levels of inter-relational accountability and intra-relational accountability in your marriage. If your ratings are low (1-3) or differ dramatically, discuss the challenges you each face with being accountable to each other and to another couple. If your ratings are high (4-5), discuss how this level of accountability has helped your marriage and identify additional ways to be more accountable.

Intra-relational Accountability   1   2   3   4   5

Inter-relational Accountability   1   2   3   4   5

Group:

1. Share your strategies for improving both inter-relational and intra-relational accountability with the group.

Assignment

1. Establish or join a group of two or more married couples within the Victorious Couples group with the expressed intention of

becoming accountable and holding one another accountable to improve your marriages.

2. Working with your accountability partners, establish benchmarks or standards to measure progress in various areas of your marriages. (e.g., develop and maintain a regular routine of conversation/discussion to evaluate progress, plan a game night/accountability activity and share the results with the larger Victorious Couples group)

Notes

_____

_____

_____

_____

_____

_____

_____

_____

_____

_____

_____

_____

_____

_____

_____

_____

_____

_____

_____

_____

_____

_____

CHAPTER 2

It's Hard Work

Opening Discussion:

What do you think of the concept, "Marriage is 50/50"? Do you agree? Why or why not?

once heard an expression, "A wedding takes but a few minutes, a marriage takes a lifetime." I've used that clever little phrase many times while conducting weddings, and it always draws smiles of affirmation from the crowd. There is a great deal of truth in those words. Our wedding ceremony, in July 1977, lasted slightly less than one-half hour. Little did we know that over 40 years later we would still be working on our marriage. I can almost hear you gasping, "Do you mean your marriage is not perfect yet?" I'm afraid not! Both Lael and I have often said that marriage is the hardest thing we've ever done, despite having faced many daunting challenges in other areas of our lives over the years. Anyone who wishes to have a successful marriage must be prepared to put hard work into it. Successful marriages do not just "happen"; rather, they take sacrifice, effort, perseverance, and God's love. A couple of expressions of unknown origin come to mind when thinking about effort in marriage: "Anything worth having is worth fighting for" and "Marriage isn't for the faint of heart".

One thing that must be eradicated early on in a marriage is laziness. The Bible says that laziness leads to poverty (Proverbs 6:6-11), and I believe that any area of life in which one is lazy will yield poverty in that same area. Consider this: Communication requires effort. Listening requires effort. Being intentional about meeting the needs of one's spouse requires effort. The extent to which we are lazy in any of these (or other) areas is the extent to which we will be in poverty in those areas. Hollywood and the internet sometimes paint unrealistic pictures of what marriage is, and what it takes to be successful in one. We see couples who look totally carefree as they live an easy life of wedded bliss on Facebook. However, these images are merely portrayals of what others want the world to see, not necessarily their reality. For example, when young women in conversation tell my wife that their friends have a perfect relationship or marriage based on postings they see on social media, Lael's favorite response is, "But it doesn't tell you that one of them cheated just two months ago." Now, this isn't to say that people shouldn't celebrate their joy in relationships. But it helps to bring realism to those who think relationships are supposed to be "perfect". Such carefree images suggest that little real work is needed to have a successful marriage, which tacitly encourages us to function in laziness. Unfortunately, many people never move beyond these unrealistic images of marriage and suffer years of being unfulfilled, dissatisfied, or worse.

A few years ago, as we were counseling a young married couple, one of them accused me of being unfair because, at that moment in time, I was asking more of one spouse than the other. The accuser made their case by insisting that marriage was supposed to be 50/50. In other words, don't ask more of me than you ask of my spouse in this (or any other) situation. After the counseling session ended,

I heard a voice speak to me with instructions to tell every married couple from that point forward: Marriage is not 50/50, it is 100/100. You see, it is the world's influence and human nature that insists that every situation requires absolute fairness and that each individual is responsible for a particular portion of the effort and nothing more. The notion of 50/50 allows us to stop when we've given what we think is the equivalent of the other party's effort. Nothing could be further from the truth. Consider the human body; each organ, muscle, artery, cell, and gland must give 100% to keep the body functioning effectively. In fact, when any part of the body breaks down, the other parts increase their output to compensate for the malfunction. Further, we all know that God's math is not the same as man's math: two shall become one (Ephesians 5:31), 2 fish + 5 loaves = 5,000+ meals (Luke 9:10-17). So, since marriage has been God's idea from the very beginning, we can't enter with our own mathematical formula that if I give exactly half, and my spouse does the same, we will be just fine.

There will be many days when one or both of you doesn't feel like giving anything. You still love each other, but the cares of life or human nature get in the way and prevent one from giving their all. That is when one person will be required to give 100% to keep the relationship working. This is important because our sense of "fairness" or "entitlement" will press us to expect at least as much in return for what we're giving. Starting today, both husband and wife should each decide to give 100% without regard to their spouse's contributions. This is the beginning of a victorious marriage.

Discussion

Group:

Now that this chapter has dismissed the idea of a 50/50 relationship, what are your thoughts of giving 100/100 in the marriage? Do you agree or disagree? In theory, 100/100 may sound like a good idea, but as flawed beings, there are times when one or both of you are unwilling to give 100%. Can you still embrace this concept and give 100%? (This will require prayer and God's grace.)

Couple:

1. How long do you typically go without speaking after an argument? In what ways can you both reduce that time to less than three hours? (This will require sacrifice from both parties and likely not a 50/50 sacrifice.)

2. What is your own (not your spouse's) biggest hindrance to having a happy home?

Assignment

1. Identify four (two each) areas in your marriage where each of you could give more than 50% of the effort toward solving a problem.

2. Ask your spouse to identify areas in the marriage where they can admit to personal laziness. Be honest and non-defensive; take turns confessing that stuff. A little honesty here will go a long way toward eliminating the scourge of laziness in your lives.

Notes

_____
_____
_____
_____
_____
_____
_____
_____
_____
_____
_____
_____
_____
_____
_____
_____
_____
_____
_____
_____
_____
_____
_____
_____
_____
_____

CHAPTER 3

Your Home, Your Church

Opening Discussion:

Describe the roles of Pastor and First Lady
in your ideal church.

God was very intentional about how He set up the marriage and family structure. We're all familiar with the roles God ascribes to husbands and wives. He makes it abundantly clear that there are spiritual roles each must assume to maintain a Christ-centered relationship and household (Ephesians 5:23). Pay particular attention to how the husband/wife relationship is modeled in the same manner as our Lord's relationship with the church.

"For we are members of His body, of His flesh and of His bones. For this reason a man shall leave his father and mother and be joined to his wife, and the two shall become one flesh. This is a great mystery, but I speak concerning Christ and the church." (Ephesians 5:30-32)

There is a profound similarity between marriage and church. It is our contention that every marriage is a mini-church, and must balance the delicate intermingling of religion and relationship. Let's consider this notion in more detail.

Many Christians believe that the New Testament is more about relationship than religion. They believe that the atoning death of our Lord and Savior Jesus Christ freed us from the rules, laws, and rituals of the Old Testament. Many speak about our freedom in Christ, and delight in the fact that we have been set "free indeed" (John 8:36). They further stress that our time as God's children should be spent developing an intimate relationship with God the Father without the burden of religious rules and regulations. This interpretation is not incorrect. However, I would pose the following question: Can anyone truly develop a relationship without some religiosity?

While it is true that we now have direct access to God in a way that the Old Testament did not allow, I believe that religion (i.e., rituals, rules, regulations) is essential in our efforts to get close to God. Let's consider a dictionary definition of the term "religion" (paraphrased from Merriam Webster):

> A fundamental set of beliefs **and practices** generally agreed
> upon by a person or number of persons (emphasis mine).

Take a look at the following New Testament scriptures:

- Pray without ceasing... (1 Thessalonians 5:17)
- ... Bless those who curse you, and pray for those who despitefully use you. (Luke 6:28)
- Therefore submit to God. Resist the devil and he will flee from you. (James 4:7)

God commands each of the above rules (religious activities) with the express intent of fulfilling a glorious relationship with Him and one another. Thus, if God requires religious activities to benefit His church, the same should apply to our marriages. Religion is essential to fulfillment in our marriages!

In reality, all of our relationships (family, co-workers, siblings, parents, employers, etc.) have certain rules and rituals that enhance or benefit those relationships. Are we not required to fulfill certain tasks as a condition of our employment? Aren't there certain expectations placed on us in our friendships and relationships with family and others? Of course, there are. These tasks and expectations are religious activities designed to enhance our relationships in life. Such is also the case in marriage. We must be intentional and very religious to fulfill our marriage relationships. That means doing things when we don't feel like doing them. That means setting aside time for the benefit of the relationship, even when it's not convenient. Husbands and wives are pastors and first ladies of their own mini-churches and must be religious about developing them to their fullest potential in God.

Discussion

1. What types of rituals did you have in your family home while growing up?
2. How did you feel about those rituals?
3. What are some rituals you would like to develop/continue in your own family?

Assignment

1. Establish a weekly dating agreement. Your date does not require a monetary expense, but must take place outside of your home, and must occur every week.
2. Establish dinner (or breakfast or lunch) times together at least 3-4 days each week.

3. Establish regular times of fellowship (as a couple) weekly. These could include prayer, scripture reading, intimacy, etc.

If you have children, develop some regular family routines that you engage in religiously as a group. This will leave a legacy that will last several lifetimes.

Notes

CHAPTER 4

Why Were We Born?

Opening Discussion:

Do you believe that everyone on earth has a pre-determined purpose in this life? If so, do you know why you were born?

There is a multitude of books, articles, and sermons on the topic of purpose. In fact, it would be overwhelming to capture all the aspects of finding one's purpose, given the fact that there is an element of faith needed to walk in one's true calling or purpose. This chapter will attempt to distill the basic elements of discovering our purpose and how our purpose relates to marriage and the family.

In John 18:37, Jesus speaks a truth that should be relevant to every believer. When asked by Pilate if He was a king, Jesus responded in so many words, "I am a king and this is exactly why I was born." We believe that every one of us who believes that we are joint heirs with

Christ (Romans 8:17) ought to have the same testimony that our Lord claimed on that fateful day before Pilate. At some point in our spiritual development, we should all be able to declare the reason for our birth and what His purpose is for our lives.

We teach that each of God's children has a purpose and destiny, and all of us were created to fulfill that purpose and that destiny. As His children, we are His most precious creation, fearfully and wonderfully made for His good pleasure (Psalm 139:14, Philippians 2:13). And as we all know, God doesn't waste any of His valuable resources (see Matthew 14:20, Mark 6:43 and Luke 9:17). Thus, His investment in creating us was not wasted, but intentional for specific reasons. The problem is that many Christians have little idea of their eternal purpose, and even less of a clue how to determine such a thing. Because of the profound differences between men and women, this dilemma may be compounded in marriage (more about that in Chapter 9).

We have developed a simple three-step process to determine one's eternal purpose. We like to use this as a guide into spiritual self-awareness, hoping it will open doors for even greater growth and discovery! Two points of clarification are important right here: (1) many people can (and often do) have multiple purposes, and (2) it is possible for one's purpose to evolve or change over time. The most important aspect in all of this is that we seek the Lord to refine and shape our purpose as we grow in His grace and wisdom. We describe the three steps below. Keep in mind that all three criteria must be met to determine a true purpose or calling from God.

1. **Identify:** What am I good at?

   To start talking about purpose, one must first answer this basic question. In all honesty, we can't have a solid conversation about the purpose of God for anyone's life without first determining that gift or talent at which they are really good. It seems obvious, but should not be taken lightly. Why would the Lord call you to something that you're really not very good at accomplishing? I know many people who want to be used as singers in the Kingdom who, for any number of reasons, are just not musically gifted. We can say the same of preachers, counselors, intercessors, drivers, cooks, butchers, bakers, and candlestick makers. God gives certain gifts, talents, and abilities to His people for His purpose and it is our responsibility to function within those areas. So, if you're not good at it, it's likely not your purpose.

2. **Determine:** What am I really passionate about?

   By that we mean, what work do you love to do? Or, what work would you do for zero compensation or recognition? This is very important because there are jobs and callings in the Kingdom that may not be very visible and God needs passionate folks willing to work without being seen or paid to fill those jobs. There are things at which one may be very good but they may not be passionate about them. An example might be that of a church musician. There are countless church organists and pianists who are excellent at what they do, but not passionate–and wouldn't consider playing without compensation. They may very well love music, but not the Godly responsibilities associated with leading God's people into worship. Likewise, there are those who are gifted church administrators and organizers who may do it for the recognition. These are all very fine people but are likely not functioning in their Godly purpose. To clarify, I'm not suggesting that they are not paid for their work, I just want to know if they would *be willing to* work without compensation. This can be a powerful test. This is not to say you won't get weary in your passion; sometimes you may even take a break for a bit. However, you will feel a tug or inner satisfaction when you get back to that thing to which you were called. I like to tell young Christians that finding one's passion is a good road map toward finding one's purpose.

3. **Clarify:** Does the activity in which I'm involved bear fruit?

In John 15:1-8, Jesus speaks to us about bearing fruit. He speaks in some detail to us about how much the Father wants us to bear more fruit and eventually, much fruit. To think about this in a more practical way, let's consider trees for a moment. Trees go through seasons ranging from dry and lifeless in the wintertime to lush and fruitful in the warmer months. Consider how joyful we all become with the return of spring and the beautiful blossoms developing on our trees. Likewise, anytime God's people bloom and blossom, it is a time of great joy in the Kingdom! As the sweet and nourishing fruit grows on the trees, the work we do for Him should produce valuable and tangible results. The work we do and the lives we live should bless the church and those around us. Undoubtedly, we have all witnessed some work being done, or some ministry performed in the church that has truly blessed the entire Body. It leaves a lasting impression in the spirits of those who were recipients. This is fruitful work. Without fruit, we can hardly say that we're functioning within our purpose.

Now that we've identified the three elements necessary to determine our God-given purpose, it's important to talk with our mates about our individual purposes and from there develop a plan through prayer for a joint and/or family purpose. This idea may be new, and some may struggle with identifying what we think our purpose might be. If your response is "I don't know" or "I can't think of anything". This is the time to go back to the first two elements. It may be something that seemed trivial, was minimized, or thought to be insignificant.

In our own lives, for example, we have a ministry to young people where I've always been passionate about feeding them spiritually and naturally. And God has blessed us with a wonderful combination of gifts as husband and wife: PJ is gifted to expound on the Word and Lael is a gifted hostess and cook. Through our purpose, the young people in our care have been blessed to be fed both spiritually and naturally. This ministry has left a permanent mark on their lives and has served as a catalyst for eternal change in many. Yes, sometimes we feel weary but the growth and fruit we see inspire us to continue each week. The result is that much fruit has come through our working together—our individual purposes have joined to fulfill an even greater purpose upon which we have built our ministry.

Discussion

Share what you learned from the lesson. Did the lesson reinforce the importance of finding purpose and, did it give you enough information to begin finding your purpose?

Assignment

1. Think of someone in your life that you believe is fulfilling their purpose in God. This person must meet all three of the criteria mentioned above. Spend some time talking with this person to find out how they discovered their journey and purpose. What did you learn that you can apply to your life?

2. Seek the Lord and spend some time in self-reflection to determine your purpose. Be careful not to confuse gifts or callings which are attractive or admirable in others with those God has given to you. Remember the three elements needed to determine purpose:

   • Identify: What am I good at?

   • Determine: What am I passionate about?

   • Clarify: What bears fruit?

3. Get together with your partner to discuss your individual purposes and then develop one or two joint and/or family purposes. Write your ideas and visions down.

Notes

Goals

A
s educators, Lael and I often encourage our students to establish goals to help them stay on track in their academic lives. Goals are important because they provide benchmarks or guidelines to keep us focused and moving forward. I've known many bright students who failed because they lacked goals and thus established no sense of focus or direction for their lives. We can say the same of the children of God. He speaks in His Word about goals. Let's consider Philippians 3:13-15. Paul indicates that there's something more available to him and that he desires to reach it regardless of the sacrifices that need to be made. That sounds to me like Paul is speaking of pressing toward a goal he has set for himself.

Just as every person needs to establish goals to achieve success, every marriage needs the same thing. Couples should spend a lifetime looking forward to various milestones in life: the wedding, the birth of each child, the purchase of a home, and many other significant events. That said, it is a wise couple that sets goals and plans for these things in advance. Ultimately, the goal-setting process will enable us to map out a life plan, and with the Holy Spirit guiding us, live it victoriously. Remember, God said in Ephesians 3:20 that He, through us, can do far above what we could ask or think. Thus, we should think and plan big so that our Heavenly Father can do far more in us and through us.

As we know, there are two types of goals—short term and long term. God can work in both as we yield ourselves and work diligently toward achieving what we've set out to accomplish. We believe that successful marriages set both types of goals and allow God to work in all cases. We like to use the following as a general guideline to determine whether a goal is a short or long term goal:

- Short-term Goal: One hour to 2 years in duration
- Long-term Goal: More than 2 years in duration

Some may say that establishing goals is challenging because we may not know what to say or we may fear deciding. To eliminate confusion, please keep in mind what's important when discussing goals. We should develop our goals using the following three constructs:

- **Realistic:** Try not to be too lofty or impractical when establishing goals. For example, rather than say we want a million-dollar mansion as our first home, consider planning for a lower valued property and working your way up. Likewise, don't develop a goal of trying to change your spouse's personality, rather work on a goal of trying to change your patience and tolerance for his/her idiosyncrasies. Remember, goals are not wishes or dreams.
- **Specific:** One of the easiest ways to get sidetracked when establishing goals is to share ambiguous ideas or plans. If you want

to get out of debt within a certain timeframe, for example, it is better to specify which bills you want to pay and in what order. This will provide benchmarks to enable you to remain on track as you progress. It will also serve as a source of encouragement as you accomplish the smaller victories. Another way of assuring specificity is to make your goals clear and concise. Rather than say, "My goal is to have a clean house," you might consider something like, "I plan to clean one or two rooms each day until the entire house is cleaned."

- **Measurable**: Our goals must be measurable. This means that there's little value in saying, "My goal is to be a better husband or wife," without understanding how to measure such a thing. This is a good reason we should discuss our goals together as a couple. One person's view of progress might not align with that of another. Don't be shy about placing expectations upon each other because, most times, that's the only way we can measure our progress.

Discussion

Share some examples of goals and evaluate whether they are short-term or long-term and meet the three criteria of being realistic, specific and measurable. If the goals do not meet the criteria, discuss how they can be improved. (Adapted from W. Paulk, How to Study in College 7th Ed., Houghton-Mifflin, 2001.)

Assignment

1. Discuss and develop at least three long-term goals as a couple.
2. Consider several short-term goals as individuals. (We will execute several short-term goals as couples in the next chapter.)
3. Identify an individual long-term goal and discuss it with your spouse.

Notes

CHAPTER 6

The "S" Word

Opening Discussion:

Each spouse must answer separately in the group.

- Have you ever been taught the meaning of submission? What did you learn?
- In your own words, what does the word submission mean in marriage? What does it mean in your marriage?
- Does the concept of submission present any tension in your marriage?
- Does submission bring up any negative images or thoughts? What about positive thoughts?

We were married in 1977. At that time, the church was in the midst of the "Jesus Revolution" and it seemed like revival was in the air everywhere you turned. There were certain basic

Christian principles that were indelible and though many of the principles were debated and interpreted differently depending on which church or denomination one attended, one was interpreted the same everywhere: SUBMISSION. I can't tell you how many times I heard the words of Paul in Ephesians 5:22 and Colossians 3:18, reminding wives to submit to their husbands! The result of all that is a narrative that places an inordinate burden on women to submit, almost to the point of oppression.

Before all of you freak out and decide that we've lost our spiritual marbles, let's be clear about one thing: We believe that God has an established order for a Christian home which includes loving headship by the male with the support and partnership of his wife. That said, I believe that the church has gone overboard in placing the burden of submission almost exclusively on women, and has sometimes hurt individuals and marriages. I have seen preachers wield the word "submission" like a club, battering everyone in its way. This approach has left the self-esteem of many women in tatters and has caused some men to misuse their God-given authority in their homes and beyond.

Let's look at the two texts referenced above to unravel the mystery of submission. In Ephesians 5, it is clear that submission is a commandment given to both husbands and wives. As we so often do in our zeal to prove a point, many husbands take verse 22 out of context in an effort to silence their wives. Let's look at the passage in context:

> [17]Therefore do not be unwise, but understand what the will of the Lord *is*. [18]And do not be drunk with wine, in which is dissipation; but be filled with the Spirit, [19]speaking to one another in psalms and hymns and spiritual songs, singing and making melody in your heart to the Lord, [20]giving thanks always for all things to God the Father in the name of our Lord Jesus Christ, [21]submitting to one another in the fear of God.[22]Wives, submit to your own husbands, as to the Lord. [23]For the husband is head of the wife, as also Christ is head

of the church; and He is the Savior of the body. [24]Therefore, just as the church is subject to Christ, so *let* the wives *be* to their own husbands in everything.

It appears as though the thought began at verse 17, where Paul stresses the importance of understanding what the will of God is: Don't be a drunkard. Do be filled with the Spirit, with the evidence of speaking and interacting positively and joyfully with one another. Do be thankful to God—in your heart and openly. Do submit to one another in the fear of God. Wives, do submit to your own husbands because your husband is over you as Christ is over the church.

There are a few points worth noting in this passage that should inform our view of submission in marriage. First of all, Paul uses the same words when instructing us to submit to each other that he uses to admonish wives to submit to their own husbands. This, to me, indicates that the submission mandate does not discriminate between women and men. God charges both husbands and wives with the responsibility of submission. Furthermore, Paul was speaking directly to wives in verse 22. For some reason, the church feels like Paul was telling men to tell women to submit. That's not how I read it; to me, it looks like he was speaking directly to women, with a word of admonition. Women are quite capable of hearing and interpreting the Word of God, without being bludgeoned by the ones who are supposedly the "beneficiaries" of their submission. Finally, let's look at the wonderful analogy Paul uses to characterize marriage. In verse 23, he says that the husband is over the wife like Christ is over the church. When have we ever known Christ to pressure His church to submit? The opposite is usually true: He allows us, through our own free wills, to disobey and make a mess of things before lovingly saving us from our own selves. Though He instructs us and provides for us, He never demands or pressures us to "submit or else." We're getting an idea of what I think Paul already knew, husbands could learn much from following Christ's example through His relationship with His church.

The passage in Colossians 3 shares similarities with those above:

> [12]Therefore, as *the* elect of God, holy and beloved, put on tender mercies, kindness, humility, meekness, long-suffering; [13]bearing with one another, and forgiving one another, if anyone has a complaint against another; even as Christ forgave you, so you also *must do.* [14]But above all these things put on love, which is the bond of perfection. [15]And let the peace of God rule in your hearts, to which also you were called in one body; and be thankful. [16]Let the word of Christ dwell in you richly in all wisdom, teaching and admonishing one another in psalms and hymns and spiritual songs, singing with grace in your hearts to the Lord. [17]And whatever you do in word or deed, *do* all in the name of the Lord Jesus, giving thanks to God the Father through Him. [18]Wives, submit to your own husbands, as is fitting in the Lord. [19]Husbands, love your wives and do not be bitter toward them. [20]Children, obey your parents in all things, for this is well pleasing to the Lord. [21]Fathers, do not provoke your children, lest they become discouraged. [22]Bondservants, obey in all things your masters according to the flesh, not with eyeservice, as men-pleasers, but in sincerity of heart, fearing God. [23]And whatever you do, do it heartily, as to the Lord and not to men, [24]knowing that from the Lord you will receive the reward of the inheritance; for[a] you serve the Lord Christ.

To provide complete context, I believe we should start at verse 12, and continue through verse 24: Do be kind, patient and humble with one another. Do forgive one another. Do put on love, peace, and thankfulness while interacting with songs and grace in your hearts. Then he goes on to give specific instructions to various groups in the body. If you look closely, the instructions can be used interchangeably with anyone. I believe they are targeted to certain groups because of that group's tendency to not follow the precept. In other words, wives are told to submit because their natural tendency may be to take charge.

Husbands are told to love because their natural tendency may be to not express emotion. Children are told to obey parents–well, you get the idea! The bottom line is *all* of us should do *all* that is outlined in these scriptures to live in a harmonious home.

Notwithstanding the explanation above, I say again that we do believe in Godly order in the home. Moreover, it is our belief that God has ordained certain roles in marriage, based on gender. Submission is one of the tools, designed by God, to help maintain a decent home. God expects the husband to establish authority in the home through sacrificial and loving leadership (not unlike how the Lord leads the church). God also expects the wife to respect and support the leadership of her husband. Many problems arise when a wife does not respect her husband's authority based on his shortcomings or her insecurities. The results of such mutiny can be catastrophic. Imagine how dysfunctional the church becomes without a willingness to submit to God's leadership. I've personally witnessed much destruction in churches and individual lives because of a lack of submission in the Body of Christ.

Likewise, in the home, there remains the responsibility of every wife to learn the importance and value of submitting to her husband. It's not a commandment to weakness, rather it's a call to strength. We recognize that this is not an easy task. It requires our flesh dying, our faith tested, and our will subjugated. Nevertheless, submission remains one of the foundational pillars upon which we build a Godly marriage.

Discussion

1. Talk with your spouse about household situations where you both can improve in submission. Be honest and non-judgmental and understand that God wants to bless both of you through submission.

2. What new concepts have you learned about submission?

3. Relate the concept of submission to the charge God has given to His elect in Colossians 3.

Assignment

1. Have an honest and open conversation about areas where the husband feels unsupported. Allow the Holy Spirit to lead the discussion around topics such as control, manipulation and lack of trust. Wives, be honest and open to appreciating your husband's Godly role and submitting yourself to it. Try diligently to avoid defensiveness. Remember, you are called to function as one, not to be enemies.

2. Develop what we call a 30-day submission plan. Each spouse will alternate having a designated month: January = husband, February = wife, March = husband, and so on.

3. During your designated month, each spouse should ask the other to do something that they have resisted in the past, and the submitting spouse is required to do it. For example, a wife may ask her husband to clean up his tool shed which he has refused to do in the past, and he must comply. Likewise, the husband may ask for a home-cooked meal twice a week, and she must comply. This can be fun and productive. Keep in mind this exercise stimulates submission in both partners. Your requests should not be disrespectful or inappropriate. Discuss the monthly plan and agree how to best implement it. Seek the guidance of your Group Leaders or accountability partners if you can't reach consensus in your household. The goal is to teach us how to submit one to another as the Bible says. It also will help us with short-term goal planning. This is not the time for revenge, nor freaky fantasies (smile).

4. The 30-day submission plan should be implemented for a minimum of 12 months to allow both partners multiple chances to give and receive. It should also be noted that if either of you fails to complete his/her task during your designated month, we ask that grace be extended for a do-over during the following month.

Notes

_____

_____

_____

_____

_____

_____

_____

_____

_____

_____

_____

_____

_____

_____

_____

_____

_____

_____

_____

_____

_____

_____

_____

_____

_____

_____

_____

_____

CHAPTER 7

Do Only Husbands Have To Love?

> ### Opening Discussion:
>
> Without using any resources, each couple is to name as many attributes of love as defined in I Corinthians 13 as they can. Discuss what these words mean.

I doubt there's a Christian husband alive who is not familiar with Ephesians 5:25 which instructs husbands to love their wives as Christ loved the church and gave Himself for her. While there are several facets to this scripture which deserve close examination, let me start by saying that the mandate to love is obviously not reserved for husbands only. The Bible commands *all of us* to love one another (1 John 4:7). Love is one of the foundations upon which our entire faith is built. So, why would Paul specifically call out husbands to remind them to do something that everyone in the Body of Christ is already commanded to do?

Before we answer the question above, let's consider how the Bible defines love. Paul, in 1 Corinthians 13, goes into significant detail in defining and characterizing love. Here's how Paul describes love (NLT):

- Patient and kind
- Not jealous, boastful, proud, or rude
- Not demanding of its own way
- Not irritable
- Keeps no record of being wronged
- Does not rejoice about injustice
- Rejoices whenever the truth wins out
- Never gives up
- Never loses faith
- Always hopeful
- Endures through every circumstance

As we review this list of characteristics, we can see that consistently practicing God's love could present significant challenges to even the most ardent of Christians. And don't forget to add to these challenges the fact that He commands that we love one another (John 13:34). For too long, we have viewed love as an emotional construct that is based on circumstances and/or feelings. Well, despite what Hollywood or the internet suggest, we need to understand that God's love is a command, and not a feeling. Thus, we are to love as described in the Word at all times, regardless of circumstances or feelings–not unlike how God loves us. Moreover, Paul, at the end of his eloquent characterization of love in 1 Corinthians 13, identifies the three great constructs of our Christian faith (verse 13). We should note that as great as faith and hope are in our Walk with Christ, love is even greater. Nothing beats love!

Once we understand how significant love is, we must learn how it is demonstrated in everyday practice. I am specifically referring to the relationship between love and giving. Beyond Ephesians 5:25 as mentioned above, the Bible speaks on several occasions of how love is manifested through giving. The first scripture that comes to mind is the ever-popular John 3:16, where we see how God demonstrates His love (for us) through the giving of His Son. And John 15:12-13 tells us of no greater manifestation of love than to give or lay down one's life for another.

Another example can be found in Ephesians 5:2, where Paul admonishes us to walk in love, as Christ did—and in so doing, gave Himself for us. Once again, we see that God's love is revealed through His willingness to give to those whom he loves. Similarly, I have wondered why Paul would say that God loves a cheerful (Greek translation: hilarious) giver in 2 Corinthians 9:7. Surely, we are well aware that God loves all of us, whether we give or not. Could it be that God is trying to show us the importance of giving as an outward demonstration of our love? If so, it makes sense for us to understand that scripture more as paraphrased, "When you give hilariously, you are showing your love for Me, and I love you right back for that!"

All of this context is necessary to understand why God would specifically instruct men to love their wives and to understand the importance of showing that love through giving. If you will indulge me for a moment, I'd like to make a sweeping generalization with no offense intended: When it comes to marriage, men tend to be far less giving than women. There, I said it. Please bear with me while I offer an example. When Lael and I were first married, we would take three to four-hour road trips to visit family from time to time. During highway driving, when it was time for bathroom and snack breaks, I would get my soda and chips and rush back to the car prepared to eat and run. I never even thought about the fact that my wife might be hungry; only that I, as the driver, needed to be satisfied so we could move on. My thinking at the time was that she could certainly get her own chips, and we would meet back at the car to resume the trip. As time went by, I learned (the hard way) that I should at least ask if she wanted anything before running into the store. Over time, however, I discovered a rather curious phenomenon. Often times when I asked, she would decline and then expect me to share my food upon her return to the car. I was absolutely flabbergasted! Didn't I ask you if you wanted anything? Don't you know that I'm the driver and need my sustenance? Why did you say you didn't want anything and then return asking me to share?

Through all of those road trips I learned something: Men don't do a good job of showing our love to our wives. I'm not for one moment suggesting that we don't love our wives. What I'm talking about is how we show it. I've heard many a man say he would take a bullet or fight off a would-be attacker on behalf of his wife. What I'd like to know is how many of us would kill or fight off *our own flesh* on behalf of our wives? This is a far more likely scenario than any external physical attack. God's love is not selfish. Jesus said the greatest love is laying down one's own life for another. Paul says love your wife as Christ gave Himself for the church. God singled men out to admonish us in an area where we are weak. I have often said that God knew what He was doing when He gave women the ability to nurse newborn babies. Try to imagine for one moment if that task were left up to men.

Discussion

1. How do you think God feels about "falling in love"? Do you think it's possible to fall *out of love* with your spouse? Consider this: Why is it we never hear of falling in or out of love with our children, but only hear of it as it relates to husbands and wives?

2. What does the Bible say about "falling in love"?

Assignment

A word of caution before beginning this assignment. There is a tendency to become defensive when asking our partner to point out areas that need improvement. Many times, our first response is to counter or deny the statement. The challenge is to accept what is being addressed. Before you start, make a mental note to put all defenses down. Be open to the very real possibility that changes are needed.

1. Husbands, write specific areas where you could help your wife and demonstrate your love for her. Wives, you write specific areas where you would like your spouse to help you that would make you feel loved. Now, wives write specific areas where you could help your husband and demonstrate your love for him. Husbands, this time you'll write areas where you would like your spouse to help you that would make you feel loved. These areas can include things in the home, they can be physical, mental or emotional. If you are having difficulty with identifying areas, just brainstorm. You can edit your list when reviewing it with your spouse. After completing your lists, compare with your spouse's. Remember to keep a check on any defensiveness. What are the differences and similarities between the two lists? Were there any items that surprised either of you on the two lists?

2. Considering what you have learned from question #1, make a list of new ways you can show love to your spouse.

3. In your prayer time, commit to giving to your spouse with joy.

Notes

CHAPTER 8

Are You A Giver?

Opening Discussion:

NOTE: *There is no judgment allowed in the following exercise. Just be honest with your interpretation of the challenge. Everyone should take a piece of paper and write down your selections in order. Then begin the discussion.*

Place the following in priority order based on your attention or focus (highest to lowest): **parents, God, children, church, spouse, job, siblings**. What criteria did you use to order your selections?

n the last chapter, we went into some detail regarding the husband's responsibility to love his wife. Now we will circle back to the significance of love for *both* partners, with a particular emphasis on giving to each other. Recall that we mentioned how God expresses His unconditional love toward us through giving (John 3:16, Ephesians 5:2).

This is a very important aspect of marriage, which is often overlooked as we become more involved in life, family and ministry.

Over the years, we have seen countless married couples who are dedicated Christians in the church struggle with making their marriages a priority. The result is a lot of unhappy Christian households and a divorce rate in the church which rivals that of the world. Many ask, "How can this be?" Well, let's consider the following scripture:

> [9]He said to them, "All too well you reject the commandment of God, that you may keep your tradition. [10]For Moses said, 'Honor your father and your mother'; and, 'He who curses father or mother, let him be put to death.' [11]But you say, 'If a man says to his father or mother, Whatever profit you might have received from me is Corban—' (that is, a gift to God), [12]then you no longer let him do anything for his father or his mother, [13]making the word of God of no effect through your tradition which you have handed down. And many such things you do." (Mark 7:9-13)

Here we find Jesus sharply criticizing the Pharisees because of their perversion of God's word to suit their purposes. Specifically, Jesus refers to the concept of "Corban" and how their use of that concept nullified God's Word and purpose. To understand this, we need to examine the Jewish customs associated with Corban (in Hebrew: Korban or Qorban). In simplest terms, Corban means a gift or offering consecrated irrevocably to God. Once Corban is declared, the gift becomes off-limits for any other purpose. By invoking Corban in this case, the Pharisees were able to circumvent the command to take care of their elderly parents (or anyone else for that matter) by saying in so many words, "what was meant for you, we will give to God." While this sounded righteous, it was a slick way to avoid having to sacrifice and care for those in need who were among them. Whatever funds or material goods that would have been devoted to helping those people were given to the church, usually to the benefit of the Pharisees, because they managed the church. The result was that the church was full, while the elderly and others in need were destitute. Meanwhile, the Pharisees felt justified because they were giving to God.

So how, you ask, does all of this Corban stuff have anything to do with unfulfilled marriages in today's church? Notice at the end of the passage Jesus says "and many such things you do." The deceptive use of Corban is not limited to the repurposing of money only. It is our firm belief that many Christian couples in our time practice Corban regularly. Any time we make church work a priority over our marriages, we are as guilty as the Pharisees. For example, is a wife's reaction the same when her husband asks her to make a special dessert some evening as when the Pastor asks for a donation of a special dessert that same evening? Would a husband be as willing to listen to his wife's burdens over breakfast as he would be to listening to the Christian brothers' burdens at a men's prayer breakfast? Do we sit on the phone and listen to church concerns but resist the thought of sitting in our living rooms and listening to our spouse's concerns?

Basically, are we taking what should be given to our spouses and giving it to the church? If so, we are guilty of declaring Corban in our marriages.

We can reveal another example of Corban in our marriages through our finances. I know of many men who are solid tithe payers but refuse to spend any "extra" money on their wives. Or, some give to the church building fund but resist spending on household improvements. A wife may buy a "thinking of you" card for a church member, yet won't buy one for her husband. This is Corban.

Let's be clear, we are not suggesting that church work should not be a priority. Nor are we minimizing how important giving or sacrificing is to building the Kingdom. All of God's people should give to the work of the Lord on this earth. However, our marriages should not suffer because of our church work. God is trying to make us givers, whether it's time, money, talent, attention, or whatever. This means we should be willing to give in every circumstance—whether at home or in the church.

Jesus puts it this way:

> "Woe to you, scribes and Pharisees, hypocrites! For you pay tithe of mint and anise and cummin, and have neglected the weightier matters of the law: justice and mercy and faith. These you ought to have done, without leaving the others undone." (Matthew 23:23)

In this scripture, our Lord is reminding us that how we treat others is just as important as how we treat God and the church: God, through the church, receives our tithe and faith, and other people receive our justice and mercy. (And I would add that for those of us who are married, "other people" most certainly includes our spouses.) As you can see, He's not suggesting that we stop giving to the church. Rather, Jesus is reminding us it's important to do both: give to the church and treat other people properly. Let's resolve to become givers in all things!

Discussion

Corban may be challenging to address in marriage because it often takes a revelation from the Holy Spirit for us to understand it. We may not be able to see our failure in this area at all when first presented with the situation. In addition, this can be an issue that's difficult to determine a right or a wrong. Because we are serving God, the argument goes, such service should not be questioned or challenged. As well, when a spouse shows more justice, mercy, and understanding to those outside the home, it can be painful to witness. It is important for everyone to remember that we all have faults and imperfections. Keep in mind all the aspects of love referenced in the last chapter. Try to maintain a light atmosphere when approaching this issue. Consider a cheerful or humorous approach. Stay prayerful as you work through this process.

Now, each couple should think back over the time you've been married and in the church. List at least four ways (two each) that you have practiced Corban. Identify ways you can resolve these practices and work together to bless the home as well as the church.

Assignment

Work together to develop a financial plan that includes giving to the church, your household, and each other. Plan to set aside a little fund for personal enjoyment for your spouse.

Notes

CHAPTER 9

That Darn Rib

Opening discussion:

Why do you think men and women are so different?

Think of instances when you and your spouse just couldn't agree on an issue. This chapter will examine and hopefully answer some puzzling questions as to why it seems our spouse is from another planet.

The first time I heard of a married couple getting a divorce, the term used to justify their breakup was "irreconcilable differences." I was young at the time and had no idea what those words meant. Over the years I've come to realize that it's a catch-all phrase to attempt to explain the fact that a husband and a wife could not get along, so they split up.

Now that we've been married for over 40 years, and have counseled many couples for over 30 years, we've experienced and seen lots of irreconcilable differences. I would argue that every marriage is full of irreconcilable differences. I have often wondered why it seems that men and women seem to disagree so often, particularly in marriage.

It all started with Adam and Eve. Let's take a look at the very first marriage to provide some insight into our irreconcilable differences:

> [21]And the Lord God caused a deep sleep to fall on Adam, and he slept; and He took one of his ribs, and closed up the flesh in its place. [22]Then the rib which the Lord God had taken from man He made into a woman, and He brought her to the man. [23]And Adam said: "This *is* now bone of my bones and flesh of my flesh; she shall be called Woman, because she was taken out of Man." [24]Therefore a man shall leave his father and mother and be joined to his wife, and they shall become one flesh. (Genesis 2:21-24)

God, in His infinite wisdom, chose to create man from the dust of the ground according to Genesis 2:7. Afterward, He created woman in an entirely different way. Instead of following the same procedure that He used to create man, God put Adam to sleep, extracted a rib from his side, and created Eve from that extracted rib. We've heard many speculations about why God chose to take the woman from the man's side: She's neither over nor under him, but beside him; she came from a place next to his heart, etc. Beyond those romantic speculations, we see a much more profound methodology if we examine the scriptures carefully. The first thing to consider is that Adam had nothing to do with how Eve was made. The fact of the matter is that Adam was sedated at the time Eve was made. Interestingly, until this point, God had involved Adam in nearly all aspects of managing the Garden of Eden. Adam was responsible to tend and keep the Garden (verse 15), and to name all the animals that God created (verse 19). Yet God gave Adam no opportunity for input about what characteristics the woman would possess. (How often we try to change our spouses into what we want them to be, instead of accepting them as God made them! We, like Adam, had no input into how they were created.)

Secondly, we need to look at God's use of Adam's rib to create Eve. Verse 21 says that God extracted the rib from Adam and immediately stitched up the incision. God removed a part of Adam to create a wife for him. Think about it, God could have used a part of Adam that would naturally regenerate such as hair or fingernails or even some internal organs, but He chose to remove a rib without replacing it. This says that Adam's wife was made from a part that no longer belonged to him. The rib would never grow back. Adam became a husband that was missing something that his wife now possessed. This is most profound when we consider how our spouse's approach to situations is almost always diametrically opposed to our perspectives. That's because the wife has something that's not in the husband, and the husband is missing something that is in the wife. Therefore, it stands to reason that we will always have irreconcilable differences—we're made differently and can therefore never be the same. Adam made it clear when he declared (paraphrased) in verse 23, "We're made from the same stuff, but she has something that was taken from me! In other words, she has something that I don't have."

Have you ever argued with your spouse and valiantly tried to get him/her to see your perspective? Have you ever thought your spouse must be nuts because he/she can't understand your approach? It is probably fair to say that there may be some things your spouse will never get about you. And it's all because of that darn rib!

Finally, verse 24 brings the entire marriage experience into perspective. Since we know that God removed something from the husband to make the wife, it is understandable that when they unite in matrimony, the two become one. However, it doesn't happen overnight. God, in His infinite wisdom, is patient and understanding with us because He knows that we have a deeply ingrained sinful nature to overcome. Likewise, when we get married, we have years of "singleness" and selfishness to overcome as we work toward oneness with our spouses. The scripture says they "shall become" one flesh. There is no way to determine how long the "becoming" process will take. That's why God says love is patient. Please don't stress over your spouse's slowness to change. Pray for them and ask the Lord for grace to deal with him/her, because he/she is in the "shall become" stage.

Oneness is God's plan for every married couple. Each partner has a portion of the whole: Adam was the original body minus the rib, and Eve was the new creation from that missing rib. When the two are joined, the result is one glorious flesh.

When we as couples work together as one, there is nothing we can not accomplish. It's a glorious mystery that is so often clouded by efforts to change one another. God made each of us who we are. We are each unique and have individual characteristics that, when joined, make both of us complete. This mystery gives us insight into a universal lesson: learning to accept and love one another despite our differences.

Discussion

1. We have all had issues in marriage that never reached an agreement or resolution. What are the ways you have handled irreconcilable differences in your marriage?

2. How can we become more spiritually proactive in dealing with our differences? In what ways can we include God's wisdom in our most frustrating moments?

Assignment

1. Each of you is to make a list of what you believe are the top three differences between the two of you. Do this separately and then come together to compare notes.

2. Discuss two or three things with your spouse you'd like to change about yourself in the marriage.

3. After completing the first two assignments, each of you resolve that there may be many aspects of your spouse that will require your acceptance. Pray together and ask God for the grace to do so.

4. Each of you should devote some of your individual prayer time to handing over those frustrating issues to the Lord. Ask God to open your spiritual eyes to see your spouse differently. Then focus on moving forward with all that God has for you.

Notes

CHAPTER 10

Active Listening:
The Key to Effective
Communication

Opening Discussion:

What's the difference between listening and hearing?
Give examples of each.

O

f the many challenges facing married couples, one of the most prevalent seems to be difficulty communicating. As we learned from the last chapter, men and women do not think alike. When they come together to run a household or raise children, communication problems become inevitable. Unfortunately, most people do not understand the amount of effort it takes to communicate effectively. Poor communication can lead to arguments, misunderstandings, and ultimately shut down by one or both spouses. To avoid these problems, we must learn the essentials of good communication.

Active listening is essential for effective communication in general, and especially in marriage. You may have heard some version of the old expression, "God gave us two ears and one mouth; therefore, we should listen twice as much as we speak." There just may be some truth to that little saying. God speaks to us through His Word about interpersonal communication and provides valuable instruction on the matter. Consider the following scriptures:

- So then, my beloved brethren, let every man be swift to hear, slow to speak, slow to wrath... (James 1:19)
- Therefore we must give the more earnest heed to the things we have heard, lest we drift away. (Hebrews 2:1)

Both scriptures address the matter of active listening, even though they don't use the actual term. In James, we are advised to use our ears first before using our mouths, which I believe will, most times, mollify our quick tempers. The writer of Hebrews addresses active listening directly, recognizing that without it we are likely to forget or overlook the very thing we were supposed to be listening to. These scriptures can provide valuable guidance regarding communication in marriage.

While we hear many things in our daily lives, I would argue that we spend very little time and energy actively listening to any of them. To clarify, *hearing* is picking up sounds as we go about our daily routine. Hearing is a passive activity that occurs because we are in reasonable proximity to the source of the sound. *Active listening*, however, requires effort and energy. According to Dr. Walter Pauk, Professor Emeritus from Cornell University, "Being a good listener means being an active listener. But listening is not the same as hearing. [Active] listening is a conscious activity based on three basic skills: attitude, attention, and adjustment." (Pauk, p. 219). We need to slow our thoughts and train our focus on the source to listen actively. Active listening can be useful in all aspects of our lives. Whether as an employee, student, friend, or church worker, being an active listener will cause us to be a better listener.

Most people spend very little time actively listening. Much of the time we engage in conversation is spent preparing a self-promoting response. To illustrate this, let's look at the following hypothetical conversations:

> **Me:** I just bought some shoes online.
>
> **Friend 1:** I hate shopping online.
>
> **Me:** It's March and we're excited about seeing our grandkids this summer!
>
> **Friend 2:** You're lucky. Our grandkids won't be here until Thanksgiving.
>
> **Me:** It's really cold outside today.
>
> **Friend 3:** Man, I love cold weather!

Which of my friends above practiced active listening? If you said none, you are absolutely correct. All of my friends *heard* what I was saying, but their energy was dedicated to turning the conversation back to themselves. This happens ALL THE TIME. If you don't believe me, I challenge you to test it for yourself. Strike up a conversation with a neighbor, friend, coworker, or relative and watch what happens. There will probably be zero active listening and lots of effort devoted to self-promotion. So, what does all of this have to do with our marriages?

Marriage magnifies the problems associated with a lack of active listening. Simple conversations between husband and wife get blown way out of proportion often because neither person listens actively. Like the conversations with my hypothetical friends, our conversation time is focused on getting back at the other person or "having the last word." We talk *at* each other and not *with* each other. We display the same self-promotion as above but add the emotions and attitudes associated with marriage into the situation. This can create an atmosphere wherein we eventually stop speaking altogether. The long-term result is that many couples exist in the same household with little or no communication between them. And when there is some issue that needs to be discussed, an argument ensues and the cycle begins again. This is where we need the grace and mercy of God in our lives.

Remember, we cannot listen actively and speak at the same time. We must practice active listening. Let's resolve to use our ears at least twice as much as our mouths.

Discussion

1. Break up into groups of twos (not with your spouse) and practice listening without turning the conversation back to yourself. (It may be more difficult than you think.)

2. Think about a time when you risked vulnerability and opened up to someone and they did not listen to you. Describe the situation and how it made you feel.

3. Think about a time (either today or earlier in your life) when you felt someone listened to you. Describe how you felt during and after the conversation.

Assignment

1. Set aside 30 minutes each day (preferably over dinner or early evening) for the next two months to have meaningful conversations and practice active listening with your partner. You might start by asking each other something as simple as "How was your day today? Tell me the highs and the lows."

2. Start a few conversations over the next few weeks with friends or coworkers to measure how little active listening is occurring in your environment. Go home and share your experiences with your spouse.

Notes

Leaving A Legacy

Although this book is focused on the marriage relationship, those of us who are parents have an additional responsibility for providing for our families–both present and future. This is emphasized in scripture more than once, but for this chapter, I would like us to focus on just one verse in particular:

A good man leaves an inheritance to his children's children... (Proverbs 13:22a)

For this discussion, we will consider the use of the word "man" to be a generic reference to both men and women. And, our focus will be on two words in that verse: good and inheritance.

"Good" is translated from the Hebrew word *towb*, (Strong's H2896) and is the same word used to describe God in Psalm 73:1. As such, it seems reasonable to define the same word used in Proverbs 13:22a as God-like or Godly. The writer of Proverbs is describing a person who is striving to be like God.

"Inheritance" is translated from the Hebrew word *nachal*, (Strong's H5157) which is used some 61 times in the old testament. Interestingly, *nachal* is a verb, not a noun. It is an action term which means "to cause to inherit". Someone must take some action to cause another person to receive the result of that action. This will become clearer if you allow me to paraphrase Proverbs 13:22a considering its literal roots:

> A person who desires to be Godly, intentionally causes his/her grandchildren (offspring) to receive an inheritance.

Although a casual reading of that scripture may bring monetary gain to mind, we will not be focusing on finances in this chapter. Not that leaving a financial legacy is not important. In fact, we believe that God intends for his people to prosper so we can leave our loved ones financially secure. But for now, we will focus on another inheritance we should prepare to leave–a Godly person creating and leaving a Godly inheritance.

All of us have received inheritances from our ancestors. Whether good or bad, we are a product of family members who came before us. We are loaded with DNA from all kinds of individuals and have inherited their traits, characteristics, and idiosyncrasies. How many of us know musicians who are descendants of musicians? Likewise, we can think of preachers, alcoholics, athletes, and abusers who inherited their characteristics from a parent or grandparent. God speaks to us about children having to deal with the outcomes of the fathers' (parents') behavior (Exodus 20:5, 2 Kings 17:41, John 8:39-40). Some inheritances are passed down through DNA, while others are observed and/

or learned behaviors. We, as God's people, have a responsibility to produce a Godly inheritance to pass onto our offspring.

I recently asked one of my daughters if she could remember something about her childhood that she'd like to recreate in her own family, and she said two things: "We ate dinner together as a family at least five days per week and we said 'I love you' to each other several times every week." Those comments resonated with me for two reasons: First, because I don't remember either of those things happening in my household when I was growing up; and second, I wondered if I could have done more for my children.

As Godly parents, we must work diligently to give our children and grandchildren solid spiritual foundations which include prayer, Bible reading, love, and fellowship. It's important to develop rituals in our homes that our children can carry with them. Always remember that they will receive from us even when it's not intended. There is something about the family structure that causes behaviors, and even attitudes, to pass down through generations. And I might add, the older we get, the more we act like our parents. This can be good or bad. I think God wrote that scripture in Proverbs 13 to remind us to be intentional about preparing our inheritance. Just as one can be fastidious about creating a savings account for a grandchild, let us be encouraged to build a large spiritual account that our children and children's children can live on through eternity!

Discussion

1. Discuss some characteristics you feel you received from your own upbringing. Which of your parents do you see in yourself?

2. We encourage those of you who have children to talk about things you see in them that remind you of yourselves—good or bad.

Assignment

1. Evaluate what you've given your children in terms of a spiritual legacy. Do you allow them to make their own decision whether to pray? Do you pray as a family? Do you attend church regularly as a family?

2. Develop some rituals such as Sunday dinner, holiday gatherings, or Bible studies which can be regularly implemented and passed on to the next generation. It doesn't matter how old your children are; it's not too late to establish rituals that will impact your family for years to come.

Notes

CHAPTER 12

Sex and Money

Opening Discussion:

What percent of your disagreements
are concerning money?

We have come to the last chapter. If you will allow us to generalize here for a moment… it is our belief that no marriage book is complete without addressing the issues of sex and money. We will not dwell on these topics because there are many excellent resources available, but we want to offer a few ideas for your prayerful consideration. We are not insensitive to the importance of sex and money in marriage, particularly in younger couples or newlyweds.

According to life coach Shellie Warren in her article "10 Most Common Reasons for Divorce" (Marriage.com, March 29, 2019), sex, and money are among the top reasons married couples break up. This is not surprising. What is surprising is that many Christians don't work through these issues, especially since we already know they present significant challenges. It's like everyone knows drinking and driving are not compatible, yet many people continue to indulge in those behaviors. Fortunately, the Bible speaks to issues regarding both sex and money. And, through prayer, wisdom, and sacrifice, God will provide the grace to gain victory over these two marriage mountains.

First, let's talk about sex. We've already discussed the fact that men and women are built differently. This is the way God made us, and in His infinite wisdom, determined that we are to come together as one. So, with intimacy, spouses need to realize that what turns one spouse on may not be what turns the other one on. Wives will respond positively to the husband's willingness to help in the household, his willingness to listen and respond to her, and his creating an atmosphere wherein she feels appreciated and secure. Husbands want to feel like the wife desires him and that she respects his manhood.

Beyond these insights, I'd like to examine the *significance* of sex in marriage. Sex is for more than producing children. Why would God design sex to be so pleasurable if it served only to procreate? I believe intimacy is so pleasurable because it has a purpose in the marriage and is meant to be indulged in regularly. The Bible says in 1 Corinthians 7:2-5 that married couples should enjoy intimacy consistently unless they both agree to abstain for a specific period. Paul suggests that sexual deprivation can lead to temptation from the enemy because he understands how strong the God-given desire for sex can be. Our years of experience in life and ministry have taught us that many couples find sexual activity to be a good way to relieve stress and renew their appreciation for one another. A good encounter in the bedroom can change the atmosphere of the entire household. I like to think our desire for sex is like our desire for food: no matter how much we get at any point in time, we will want to return for more eventually. These desires are only temporarily satisfied, always needing to be replenished. This is God's design.

One recommendation we would like to offer to every couple is that together you consider putting intimacy into your schedule. That's right, pull out your planner and set aside specific days and times for physically coming together. This flies in the face of the Hollywood image of hot, spontaneous sex, but as we discussed earlier, much of what God instructs in marriage is to be done based on his commandments, not by our feelings. Since we already know what things stimulate husbands and wives sexually, why not make it a practice of doing those things all the time, understanding that by so doing, we can minimize the chances of a partner not being mentally or physically ready on your scheduled days. Believe me, this does not have to be as mechanical as it sounds. Everyone has a sex drive… why not work toward fulfilling those desires regularly at agreed-upon times? Given how hectic and busy all of our lives are, it makes as much sense to plan intimacy every bit as much as it makes sense to plan meals together.

Now, let's talk about money. The Bible speaks about money many times; most of us are familiar with some of the more popular verses (Malachi 3:10, Luke 6:38, 2 Corinthians 9:7). What's important to remember is that for Christians, dealing with money requires not only fiscal wisdom but also faith. We believe that tithing was introduced to God's people as a way of teaching us to rely on God rather than our ability to make a living. The Bible says that God owns the cattle on a thousand hills (Psalms 50:10). Thus, He doesn't need our tithes and offerings. He asks us to give to increase our faith in Him.

What happens in marriage, however, is that the husband and the wife may not have the same measures of faith. In marriage, we have two people from different backgrounds and upbringings, placed into one household with expenses and bills from everywhere. Now add two people with different measures of faith trying to manage the situation. This is a recipe for disaster! Our first recommendation is that you both pray earnestly about your finances–from all perspectives: who will manage the money, giving to the church, prioritizing of bills and expenses, trusting God, etc. We all need to remember that God will never put more on us than we can bear (1 Corinthians 10:13). He will provide wisdom and grace to get through the financial challenges as they may arise from time to time. Recall all the things we discussed in earlier chapters—compromise, communication, active listening. Now is the ideal time to put those things into practice.

There's one other issue that should be addressed concerning Christians and finances. Look at the following scripture in Ecclesiastes 7:1:

> A good name *is* better than precious ointment, And the day
> of death than the day of one's birth.

For years, when I considered this verse, I thought the first part spoke of the value of things like honesty and integrity, and the second part spoke of going to heaven when this life is over. However, while researching for this book the entire verse took on new meaning regarding finances. Here's my new interpretation after exploring the text more closely:

- The original Hebrew word translated "name" refers to reputation or report.
- The original Hebrew word translated "ointment" here means oil, and is the same word David used in Psalm 23 when he wrote "You anoint my head with oil." That anointing has to do with the ministry placed within us by God.
- This is the Message Bible translation of the second part: Your death date tells more than your birth date.

In Christian financial management, I believe God wants us to have a good reputation with our creditors (i.e., a good credit report), and he does not want us to leave our families in debt because of our passing away. I believe this lifelong good credit reputation is more valuable than any other part of our ministries. What a sad testimony to have a great preacher or prayer warrior who does not pay his/her bills! What kind of witness is that? And, how tragic for a family to deal with the death of a loved one along with the burden of his/her unresolved financial issues!

So, if you will allow me, let me rephrase the verse, and each of us to read together with our spouses next payday:

> Having good credit is better than being good at ministry, and my family will not be financially stressed because of my death.

Discussion

In the large group setting, break into two smaller groups. One group will take sex, the other will take money, then discuss the ideas presented in the chapter. Come back to together and answer the following:

1. How can we make this work for us?
2. In what ways have we failed to plan adequately for either?

Assignment

1. Try planning intimacy for one month. Discuss ways you can make it happen. Initially, this may be awkward but does not have to be difficult. You're married… enjoy this activity! Reevaluate after one month.
2. Look at your monthly budget together. Check your credit scores. Make a plan to improve them.
3. Discuss any arrangements you have made for when the Lord calls one or both of you home. Review your life insurance policies and pensions.

Notes

Afterword

Congratulations! You have completed one year of the Victorious Couples program. I suspect you have been challenged, encouraged, frustrated, and amused throughout the year. I sincerely hope your marriage relationship has been enhanced and stimulated in new ways.

As you have likely noticed, there are many scriptural references throughout this workbook. I encourage all of you to develop a regimen of consistent Bible reading and study. God has given us everything we need by His grace through His Word. Let's take advantage of everything God has for us by studying the Bible and thereby improving our walk with Him!

Now that your Victorious Couples year is over, I invite you to pray and consider starting your own Victorious Couples group. Ask the Lord to show you three or four married couples who could benefit from this program. As you know, it's an excellent way to help others while also promoting Godly fellowship and comradery. If you'd like additional information about starting a Victorious Couples group, I invite you to email us at jenkins@myvictory.org

CPSIA information can be obtained
at www.ICGtesting.com
Printed in the USA
LVHW010543291019
635545LV00008B/3640/P

9 781733 453905